CONDEMNED

Caitlin Scott

SADDLEBACK
EDUCATIONAL PUBLISHING

ASTONISHING HEADLINES

Attacked

Captured

Condemned

Kidnapped

Lost and Found

Missing

Shot Down

Stowed Away

Stranded at Sea

Trapped

SADDLEBACK
EDUCATIONAL PUBLISHING
www.sdlback.com

Copyright © 2005, 2013 by Saddleback Educational Publishing

ISBN-13: 978-1-61651-920-9
ISBN-10: 1-61651-920-7
eBook: 978-1-61247-077-1

Printed in Guangzhou, China
0712/CA21201055

17 16 15 14 13   1 2 3 4 5

Photo Credits: Cover, page 41, Shaun Walker, Zuma Press; page 9, Picture History; page 19, Bryce Flynn, Zarchive; page 58, STR/Reuters Photo Archive; pages 66–67, © Brandon Alms | Dreamstime.com; pages 76–77, © Benjamin Albiach Galan | Dreamstime.com; page 88, © Lucian Coman | Dreamstime.com

CONTENTS

What does it mean to be condemned? If a person commits a crime or does something bad, that person may be condemned.

Not everyone agrees on who should be condemned. Sometimes it is hard to know what or who is right.

For example, Giles Corey lived in Massachusetts in the 1600s. He was accused of witchcraft. Not everyone thought he was guilty. But he was condemned to death by a court.

More recently, Ray Krone was accused of a young woman's murder. He did not kill anyone. Sadly, he spent a long time in jail.

People are not the only ones who are condemned. Fierce animals are condemned too. Farmers do not want wolves to eat their animals. The farmers sometimes even kill the wolves.

Even buildings and trees get condemned. The owners of New York's Grand Central railway station wanted to tear down the building or build on top of it. Luckily, other people thought it was beautiful and wanted to save it from destruction.

People like Julia Hill want to save condemned trees. Loggers turn these trees into lumber for houses. However, if the oldest trees are cut down, it could take hundreds of years to replace them.

Do the condemned deserve their fate? Who and what should be saved?

Accused of Witchcraft
DATAFILE

Timeline

January 1692

Girls in Salem accuse others of witchcraft.

September 1692

Giles Corey accused of witchcraft. He is placed
under heavy stones and is crushed to death.

Where Salem, Massachusetts?

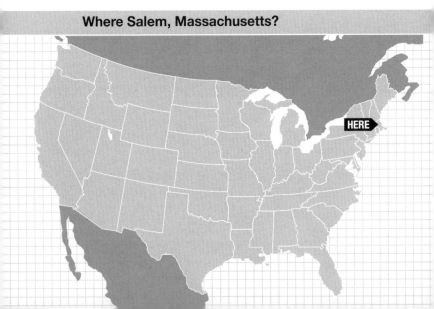

HERE

Key Terms

accusation—a charge of wrongdoing; a statement that someone is to blame

condemn—to judge as guilty or unfit

confess—to admit to a crime

hysterics—a severe attack of panic or distress

property—things that a person owns

torture—inflicting pain or hurting someone so that he or she will confess or give information

Did You Know?

In the 1600s, courts were not like our courts today. They allowed "spectral evidence." This meant someone could say that the spirit of another person was hurting them. This spectral evidence proved the accused person was a witch.

Accused of Witchcraft

The people of Salem were in hysterics. Two young girls, Ann Putnam and Abigail Williams, fell ill. They screamed and had terrible fits. Dr. Griggs could find nothing wrong.

His conclusion: It must be witchcraft!

The girls blamed some townspeople for their illnesses. They said the people's spirits tortured them. The townspeople believed the accused must be witches.

The accused were brought to trial in Salem. If they confessed to witchcraft, they were sent to prison. If they did not confess, the court most often found them guilty anyway. If the court found them guilty, they were often hung.

Witch-Hunt Victims of Salem

Accused of witchcraft: 100+

Hanged: 19

Pressed to death: 1

Died in prison: 4

A courtroom scene from one of the Salem witchcraft trials

The Accusation

In April 1692, the girls accused Giles Corey of Salem village. He was 80 years old. He was to be tried in September. Corey was very frightened. The court had already hung 11 people that summer, even though there was no real proof they were witches.

Many others were in prison. Corey's own wife, Martha, was also accused. If they were both put in prison or hung, the court might take their house and farm.

Corey gave all his property to his two daughter's husbands. But he was afraid the court might also take it from the two men. Many other people in prison had already lost their land.

The Torture

Corey was a stubborn man. Not everyone liked him. He often disagreed with his neighbors about land. And when he thought he was right, he did not back down. Corey had even taken a few men to court to settle these arguments.

As many as 12 people said Corey was a witch. Some were people he had argued with. Corey was sent to trial for witchcraft.

But Corey was different from other accused people in Salem. He kept silent. The court could not try him, because he would not talk.

This must have made the court very angry. They wanted Corey to confess to witchcraft. So they tortured him. Torture was legal back in those days.

On September 17, 1692, the sheriff and six men from Salem tied Corey up. They put him under a big board. Then, they put heavy stones on top of the board.

They asked Corey again and again if he was a witch. He would not talk, so they added more stones. They left him there all night under the heavy stones.

The next day, eight other people were condemned by the court. All eight would later hang and lose their houses and farms.

Corey was stubborn. He still would not confess. They added more stones. Corey could hardly breathe. The only thing he said was, "More weight."

All day the Salem men added large stones to the pile already on Corey's chest.

The Final Outcome

On September 19, 1692, Giles Corey was crushed to death.

Some say Corey kept quiet so that he could keep his property and pass it on to his children and grandchildren. Others say he wanted to show how stupid and unfair the witch trials were.

Was Giles Corey a witch? It is not likely. The Salem witch trials ended a year later. Everyone still in jail was set free.

Ann Putnam, one of the girls who named names, later confessed she had lied about the witches' spirits. She said she was sorry. She was the only accuser to apologize.

Should Giles Corey have been condemned? You decide.

Saving Grand Central
DATAFILE

Timeline

February 1913

Grand Central railway station opens in New York City.

October 1969

Owners battle New York City mayor to tear down Grand Central.

Where is New York City?

HERE

Key Terms

committee—a group that works together to accomplish a goal, such as saving a building

desperate—without hope; worried

landmark—a building or place that is historic or important

municipal—having to do with local or city government

press conference—a collective interview where a person answers questions from members of the press

Did You Know?

Buildings cost a lot of money to build. When Grand Central was built, it cost $80 million. Restoring it in the 1990s cost more than $190 million.

Saving Grand Central

There is nothing else like Grand Central in New York City. There is nothing like Grand Central in all of America or even in the whole world.

Grand Central is more than just a railway station. It is part of American history.

Grand Central Terminal

Grand Central is a beautiful building. It has many works of art and impressive architectural features:

- a 50 foot statue of the Greek gods Hercules, Minerva, and Mercury on the front.

- a main concourse that is 120 feet wide, 375 feet long, and 125 feet high.

- a ceiling painted with 2,500 stars by French artist Paul Helleu.

- three 75-foot arched windows.

- a double staircase made of marble, like one in a famous Paris opera house.

- an entire floor made of Tennessee marble.

An Early Morning Surprise

Imagine Jackie Onassis's surprise on a January day in 1975. She read in her morning paper that the city of New York had lost a court case to save Grand Central.

The judge said the mayor of New York had no right to tell the owners what to do. He said the owners could tear down Grand Central or build on top of it. They could do whatever they wanted. Grand Central might be knocked over and cleared away! The once beautiful building might be ruined.

Or, if it were less expensive, the owners might build a 55-story building right on top of Grand Central. The old station would not be destroyed. But, another building would cover it up.

The reason to condemn the building was simple. Grand Central's owners were losing money. They wanted a newer building with more office space. The building was condemned.

Jackie was the widow of the late President Kennedy. Jackie was very popular, and she was often seen in magazines and on TV.

Jacqueline Kennedy Onassis

Jackie thought New Yorkers might listen to her. She must have made up her mind that very day. She would try to save Grand Central!

Desperate Times

But how could Jackie help? Other New Yorkers wanted to save Grand Central, too. The Municipal Art Society had fought hard during the first trial. They had argued in court that the station should be saved. But the judge did not agree with them.

There was one thing that might help. The city mayor could still appeal the judge's decision. He could ask a higher court to retry the case. But the mayor was not sure he wanted to do that. He was afraid of another battle with the building's owners.

Grand Central's owners said they were losing $8 million a year by staying in the old building.

If they demolished the station and built a bigger building, they could have more offices inside. The owners could make more money.

If the mayor appealed, the station's owners would sue the city for lost income. The mayor had just about given up. Jackie and the other New Yorkers who loved Grand Central were desperate. How could they convince the mayor to appeal the case?

New Yorkers Fight to Save Grand Central

A few days after Jackie read the newspaper article, the Municipal Art Society's secretary got a call. It came from a woman with a quiet voice. She said she wanted to help save Grand Central. The secretary asked for the woman's name. The woman said she was Jackie Onassis.

The secretary put Jackie on hold. At first, no one in the office could believe it really was Jackie Onassis on the phone. Imagine how happy they were to know she was on their side!

Within a month, the Municipal Art Society formed a committee to save the old railway station. Jackie joined the team.

Jackie Takes Action

Jackie wrote a letter to the mayor. She told him how important it was to save Grand Central. She said the building was part of American history.

Jackie held a press conference on January 31, 1975, in New York City.

"... old buildings are important and if we don't care about our past, we cannot hope for our future." — Jackie Onassis

The mayor agreed with her. He soon appealed the case! Now it was up to the New York Court of Appeals to decide.

Another Loss, A New Trial

But the city lost in court again. This time the mayor was ready. He appealed the case at the US Supreme Court.

On April 17, 1978, Jackie held a press conference on a train. She and other New Yorkers took a train from Grand Central to Washington, DC, where the new trial would be.

Everyone on the train talked about saving Grand Central. They said the station was important to the whole country.

"If Grand Central Station goes, all the landmarks in this country will go as well...."
— *Jackie Onassis*

Victory at Last!

On June 26, 1978, the city won its court battle. The Supreme Court judges said Grand Central was a landmark. The station was saved!

Beautiful Once Again

On October 1, 1998, the station's repairs were finished. About 5,000 people came to cheer. Many thanked Jackie, who had died four years before.

Jackie Onassis will be remembered for many things. Saving Grand Central will be one of the best.

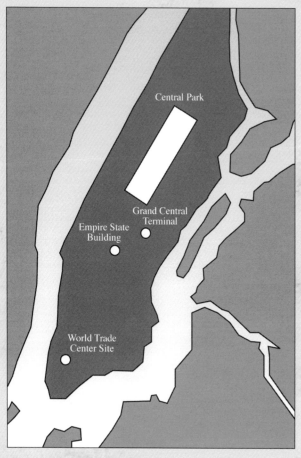

Central Park

Grand Central
Terminal

Empire State
Building

World Trade
Center Site

New York City is home to many famous buildings. The Empire State Building was once the tallest in the world. Sadly, terrorists attacked the World Trade Center. The Twin Towers fell on September 11, 2001.

Yellowstone Wolf Gunned Down

DATAFILE

Timeline

1975–1977
Study finds no wolves are left in Yellowstone
National Park. Elk have begun to overrun the park
and are destroying the natural landscape.

March 1995
Fourteen wolves freed in Yellowstone National
Park.

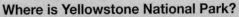

Where is Yellowstone National Park?

HERE

Key Terms

alpha female and alpha male—the strongest female and male in a pack

pack—a wolf's family group

pup—a baby wolf

rancher—someone who raises livestock

regurgitate—to vomit up food to feed young animals

Did You Know?

Wolves belong to the dog family. Foxes and coyotes are also part of this family. Do you have a pet dog? If so, your dog is also related to wolves.

CHAPTER 3

Yellowstone Wolf Gunned Down

Remember little red riding hood and the three little pigs? Small children are taught that wolves are mean and scary.

Wolves, like this one, are close relatives of dogs.

In the 1600s, wolves were condemned to death. Many people hated wolves and tried to kill them.

The Massachusetts Bay Company even paid people to kill wolves in the colonies. One wolf brought about $5 in today's money. Lots of people wanted to make money. It was easy to kill wolves. Soon, no wolves were left in the eastern part of the country.

In the 1800s, people moved west across America. Wolves and people competed to live on the same land. Ranchers started poisoning wolves. If they found an animal killed by a wolf, they would put poison in the animal. All the wolves that later ate the animal died, even the pups.

By the 1930s, there were very few wolves left alive in America.

New Facts about Wolves

But some people liked wolves. Scientists studied wolves in the wild parts of Canada and Alaska. Two scientists who studied wolves were Sigurd Olson and Adolph Murie.

Olson and Murie found that wolves were important to the cycle of life. Wolves killed old and sick animals. They kept the numbers of wild sheep and deer under control. Without wolves, there would be too many sheep and deer. These grazing animals would eat everything. Then they would starve along with other animals.

In short, wild places needed wolves.

Wolf Facts

- Grown male wolves weigh between 80–130 pounds.

- Grown female wolves weigh between 50–110 pounds.

- Wolves live up to 13 years in the wild; they live up to 20 years in zoos.

- Wolves mate for life. They change partners only if one wolf dies.

- Female wolves can have as many as 10 pups at a time.

- Pups weigh only about 1 pound at birth. They are blind and deaf when they are newborns.

- Wolves used to live in 50 US states. Now wolves only live in small parts of Washington, Idaho, Montana, and Wyoming.

From the 1940s on, scientists tried to bring back wolves to America. Many thought the best place for wolves would be Yellowstone National Park. The park was big and had lots of sheep, deer, and elk for wolves to hunt. They hoped the wolves would stay away from farms, where animals were raised.

The Wolves Return

Finally in 1995, scientists brought back wolves to Yellowstone National Park. Would the wolves like Yellowstone? Would they survive?

The scientists caught 14 wolves in Canada. They put radio collars on the wolves. These collars would tell the scientists where the wolves roamed when they were set free.

Next, they fenced in an area in the park. Here the wolves got to know each other and their new home.

A black wolf called Number Nine was the biggest female in the group. A silvery gray wolf, Number Ten, was the largest male. The scientists hoped the two would mate, but they also feared a fight.

Fortunately, the two wolves liked each other. They played and snuggled. They slept curled together. They became the alpha male and alpha female of the pack.

Soon the scientists found that Number Nine was going to have pups. They decided the time had come to set the wolves free. Late in March 1995, they opened the fence. Number Ten walked out first. He was the first free wolf in the park. The others followed his lead and headed for the wild.

Tragedy

But not everyone was happy about the return of the wolves. Some people still hated and feared wolves.

A month later, just outside the park, Chad McKittrick's truck was stuck in the mud. He had been bear hunting. He had a gun.

Up on a ridge, he saw a silver-gray wolf. He ran to get his gun and aimed. His friend, Dusty Steinmasel, thought it was somebody's dog. He told McKittrick not to shoot.

But, McKittrick knew it was a wolf. He fired. Number Ten fell dead.

If McKittrick thought he could get away with killing Number Ten, he was wrong.

The scientists were watching the signals from Number Ten's radio collar. Usually, the radio signal showed that the wolf was moving. Even when Number Ten slept, he moved a little bit. The scientists saw that Number Ten was not moving. They feared the worst.

The scientists searched for Number Ten. They found his collar in a creek. McKittrick had removed the collar. He knew it was against the law to kill a wolf. But McKittrick had not destroyed the collar. He did not think the scientists would be watching so closely.

Then, the scientists found Number Ten dead nearby. The scientists questioned everyone who lived in the area. Finally, Steinmasel talked.

McKittrick confessed. He paid a $10,000 fine and spent six months in jail for his crime.

But the punishment would not bring Number Ten back. How would Number Nine raise their pups alone?

In a wolf pack, both parents are important. One parent stands watch over the pups. The other hunts for food. The hunting parent eats really fast, runs home, and then regurgitates the food so the young can eat.

Number Nine could not watch over her pups and still go off to hunt. Without two parents, the pups might starve to death or be eaten by coyotes or bears.

If these pups died, would wolves ever live free in Yellowstone National Park?

Protecting the Pups

The scientists did not want the wolves to die. They caught Number Nine and her pups. That summer, they kept Number Nine and the pups in a pen. They brought the wolves food and made sure no one hurt them. They also brought in more wolves from Canada.

On October 11, 1995, the scientists set Number Nine and her pups free again. Number Nine and her pups thrived. She soon found a new mate and had at least four more litters in the park.

Some people may still be afraid of wolves. And sadly other Yellowstone wolves have been shot. But today, with more than 150 wolves in the park, the once condemned wolves are here to stay!

CHAPTER 4

Redwood Slated to Get the Ax
DATAFILE

Timeline

1395 or earlier
A redwood sprouted in Headwaters Forest. The sprout became "Luna."

February 1974
A little girl was born to a traveling preacher. She became "Butterfly."

Where is Headwaters Forest, California?

HERE

Key Terms

activist—a person who works for a cause

media—television, newspapers, and radio

slated—chosen for a specific purpose

tree-sitter—an activist who climbs a tree and stays up there to keep the tree from getting cut down

vegetarian meals—meals without meat

? Did You Know?

Redwoods can grow to be 325 feet tall and 12 feet across. That is longer than a soccer field and taller than your school!

Redwood Slated to Get the Ax

Headwaters Forest is one of the last "old growth" forests in America. An old growth forest is one whose trees have never been cut down. Once, old growth forests covered our country. Now only three percent of those are left.

Pacific Lumber Company owns Headwaters Forest. The lumber company wanted to cut down the trees in Headwaters Forest. Why? So they could make money. It wanted to sell the trees for lumber. The wood is turned into houses and furniture.

However, once a redwood tree is cut down, it takes hundreds and hundreds of years for another tree to grow as tall.

Luna, a 200-foot redwood tree, was one of the trees slated to get the ax.

Julia "Butterfly" Hill next to Luna, the redwood tree she occupied in an effort to save it.

Save the Forest, Climb a Tree

In 1997, Julia Hill was just out of college. She met some activists who were trying to save Headwaters Forest. She and her friends got to know the trees. They gave the trees names, such as "Everlasting Life," "Jerry," and "Luna." Luna was Julia's favorite tree.

Julia and her friends also gave themselves new names. One was called "Remedy," another "Gypsy." Julia became "Butterfly." This had been her nickname since she was a child. Her family started calling her that the day a butterfly followed her for hours.

In December 1997, the lumber company had plans to cut down more trees. Butterfly and her friends were upset. On December 10, 1997, Butterfly sneaked through the forest.

When she came to her favorite tree, she took off her shoes. Barefoot, she would not hurt Luna's bark. She could also use her feet and toes to grip the tree. Then, she climbed into Luna's high branches.

That day, Butterfly saved Luna's life. The lumber company could not cut down the tree without hurting Butterfly.

Life in a Tree

Butterfly thought she would stay up in Luna's branches for only a few days. She made a little platform. But, the lumber company still wanted to cut Luna down. They waited for Butterfly to get tired and climb down.

It was a cold, wet, and stormy winter. But Butterfly's friends helped her stay put. They brought her food and other things she needed. The days passed slowly. Soon, Butterfly and her friends built a 6-foot by 8-foot tree house. It perched 18 stories up in Luna's branches. Now, Butterfly stayed dry.

It was not easy living in a tree. The tree house did not have a bathroom. Butterfly had to use a bucket. She lowered it down to her friends. The tree house did not have a TV or computer. She could not run, ride a bike, or go to the movies. She was stuck in a tree. The lumber company hoped Butterfly would get bored.

But she did not get bored. Butterfly read books, wrote poetry in her journal, and made vegetarian meals. She got her exercise by climbing up and down Luna's branches.

Butterfly also had a cell phone. She told everyone how important it was to save the trees.

"Here I can be the voice and face of this tree, and for the whole forest that can't speak for itself."
— Julia "Butterfly" Hill

Until Butterfly's time in Luna, the world record for tree sitting was 42 days. By January 23, 1998, Butterfly broke the record! The media came from all over to talk to her.

Butterfly's quest became famous. Newspaper reporters came from all over the world to interview her.

Pop stars, such as Bonnie Raitt and Joan Baez, even visited her in the forest. Soon, Butterfly celebrated her first year in the tree.

But the lumber company still wanted to cut Luna down.

Striking a Deal

Some people thought Butterfly was crazy. But others thought she was doing the right thing. They also wanted to save the trees of Headwaters Forest.

TV and newspaper reporters told Butterfly and Luna's story to the nation. Many people became angry with the lumber company. Many supporters came and camped out in Headwaters Forest. This made it hard for the company to cut down trees. Others wrote letters and spoke against the company. The owners spent a lot of time talking to reporters in their offices and trying to get around campers in the forest.

In December 1999, Butterfly and her friends made a deal with the lumber company. The company agreed not to cut Luna down. They also agreed not to cut down any of the trees around Luna.

In return, Butterfly and other activists paid the lumber company $50,000 for Luna and her fellow trees. The lumber company gave this money to Humboldt State University. The university promised to use it to study the forest.

On the cold, wet morning of December 18, 1999, Butterfly climbed down from Luna. When her feet finally touched the ground, she knelt and kissed the earth.

She had been in the tree a long time, but it was worth it. She had saved Luna and the trees around her. She had spent 738 days off the ground. That is more than two years!

Luna was safe. But many lumber companies continue to cut down many old growth trees. The struggle between tree-sitters and lumber companies goes on.

Luna's Lifetime

—Around 1395 Luna sprouts.

—1492 Columbus arrives in America.

—1600s Colonists settle in America.

—1700s Steam engines are invented.

—1800s Forests in the east are cut down. Loggers move west. Railroads push west across the United States.

—1900s Cars and computers are invented.

—1960s Only 15 percent of old growth forests are left.

—1990s Only 3 percent of old growth forests are left.

—2000s Luna lives on!

How Tall is a Redwood Tree?

All of these trees grow in the American west. The redwood tree grows the tallest of all American trees.

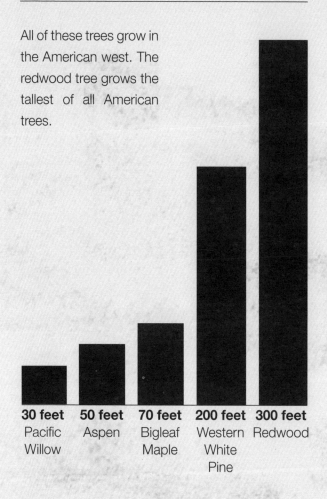

| **30 feet** | **50 feet** | **70 feet** | **200 feet** | **300 feet** |
| Pacific Willow | Aspen | Bigleaf Maple | Western White Pine | Redwood |

DNA Frees Snaggletooth Murderer
DATAFILE

Timeline

December 1991

Kim Ancona is found dead in Phoenix, Arizona.

Months later, Ray Krone is jailed for her murder.

April 2002

DNA evidence frees Krone.

Where is Phoenix, Arizona?

Key Terms

DNA—an acid that carries genetic information in a living cell

evidence—something that helps prove or establish a point in question

expert—a person who knows a lot about a topic

innocent—not guilty

Did You Know?

Some people sent to jail are innocent. DNA evidence has freed many. Ray Krone was the one-hundredth person freed with the use of DNA evidence..

DNA Frees Snaggletooth Murderer

The Victim

It was a horrible crime. Someone murdered a young woman as she cleaned up at the end of the night. Kim Ancona worked at the CBS Lounge in Phoenix, Arizona. She was a 36-year-old waitress.

The police were on the scene the next morning. They found an important clue. Ancona had bite marks on her body. Some of the bites went right through her shirt!

The police thought Kim fought back because they found blood that was not hers. This might have been the murderer's blood. Could it help them find the killer? Unfortunately, the blood was "Type O," the most common blood type of all.

The police decided they would have to use the bite marks to track down Kim's killer.

These bite marks showed that the killer had crooked teeth. The police looked for a person with crooked teeth. They thought the killer was a man. Ancona had been cleaning the men's bathroom when she was killed. The police called him the "Snaggletooth Murderer."

The Accused

Ray Krone heard about Kim Ancona's murder. He lived near the CBS Lounge. Sometimes he went there to play darts. He often talked to Kim. But Krone was surprised to learn that the police thought *he* was the murderer. Krone was a mailman. He had never committed a crime before. He had even served in the US Air Force.

None of his friends or family believed he was the Snaggletooth Murderer. Why did the police think Krone was a murderer?

Krone had crooked teeth. Snaggletooth is another name for crooked teeth. This was the main evidence the police thought they had against Ray Krone.

The Trials

In court, the police could not prove that Krone had been at the CBS Lounge that night. But, they did show a video of him. The video showed a close up of Krone's teeth. Then, it showed a bite mark on Ancona's body. Lastly, the video moved the photo of Krone's teeth over the bite mark.

It looked as if it were a perfect match. The video also looked gruesome to the jury. It was almost as if Krone's teeth were really biting Ancona.

Krone's lawyer had not known about the video before the trial. He had another expert who thought that Krone's teeth did not match the bite marks. But it was too late to call in this expert.

In the end, the jury believed the video. In 1992, Krone was condemned to death. He spent almost three years on death row in Florence Arizona State Prison. He expected to die.

Then in 1996, Krone got a retrial. His lawyer brought in the other expert, Homer Campbell. But he did not help Krone very much. The jury still believed the video. This time, Krone was sentenced to life in Yuma Arizona State Prison.

DNA Evidence

At the time of the first and second trials, DNA testing was not used very much. It cost a lot to test the evidence. Plus, DNA testing was very new. Juries sometimes did not understand or trust DNA evidence.

Over the years, as DNA evidence was used more often, Krone's family had an idea. The killer had bitten Kim Ancona through her shirt. Maybe the shirt still had saliva on it. If it did, it could be tested for DNA evidence. This idea gave them hope. In early 2001, Krone's family asked the court to do the DNA testing on the shirt.

Still, DNA testing takes a long time. The process is difficult and has to be done just right. If a tiny flake of skin or strand of hair from someone at the lab gets into the experiment, the results may be wrong.

Also, there are now many, many cases that use DNA testing. Most labs have long waiting lists. Krone and his family waited for the results for about a year.

In April 2002, when Krone's family heard from the lab, they were thrilled. Not only did the shirt still have saliva on it, but the results showed that Krone could not be the killer. Instead, the results pointed to another man.

This man, Kenneth Phillips, was already in jail for attacking a child. Phillips also had crooked teeth. Experts said Phillip's teeth matched the bite marks on Kim Ancona's shirt.

Released

Ray Krone was set free on April 8, 2002. He was happy but also a little sad. He had been in jail for ten years. He had lost ten years of his life!

"For ten years I felt less than human. This [freedom] is certainly a strange feeling, and I think it'll take a while for it to set in."
— Ray Krone

Ray Krone after his release from prison

What is DNA Fingerprinting?

James Watson and Francis Crick discovered DNA in 1953. But it was not used to solve crimes until 30 years later. The man who found a way to "map" DNA was Dr. Alec Jeffreys. But Jeffreys was not a policeman, he was a scientist.

Jeffreys found the way to "map" DNA in 1984. He used X-rays to show the patterns in DNA. This process is called DNA fingerprinting. DNA fingerprinting can match things found at the crime scene, such as blood, hair, and saliva, with the person who committed the crime.

DNA evidence was first used in a criminal trial in England in 1987.

CHAPTER 6

The Innocence Project
DATAFILE

Timeline

November 1987

One of the first criminal court cases using DNA as evidence took place in Orange County, Florida.

1989

First person exonerated using DNA evidence.

1992

The Innocence Project is founded at Benjamin N. Cardozo School of Law in New York City.

Where is Florida?

Key Terms

exoneree—a person freed from blame

misconduct—unacceptable behavior

prosecutor—a government lawyer who tries criminal cases

public defender—a lawyer employed with public money to represent a defendant who cannot afford to pay

?

Did You Know?

DNA is used in criminal investigations to identify remains, determine blood relationships, prove ownership of personal items, and to see if a certain person was in a certain location.

The Innocence Project

Barry Scheck and Peter Neufeld founded the Innocence Project in 1992. This organization works to change the justice system. The main thing they do is help prisoners get freed when DNA testing has proven their innocence. This is called DNA exoneration.

The presumption of innocence is a legal right in the United States. This means the accused is said to be innocent until proven guilty. Prosecutors have to prove guilt. If they can't, the accused person must be set free.

But often it doesn't work that way. Sometimes innocent people are sent to prison. And sometimes they are even executed. There are many reasons. Racism is one. African Americans and Latinos are more likely to be convicted of a crime. But this may be because more live in poverty. Poor people can't afford high-powered lawyers.

Sometimes a poor person gets a public defender. That is a lawyer provided free of charge. Some public defenders are inexperienced. Sometimes they have a heavy caseload. With too many cases, they can miss important details.

Innocent people often think the mistake will be cleared up quickly. So they tell police everything they know. They figure they did nothing wrong. So they have nothing to hide.

But sometimes police just want to wrap up the case. This is especially true when the crime is covered heavily in the news. Prosecutors pressure police to find a suspect. When the case is "solved," news reports make the police look like heroes. And the public feels safe again.

Sometimes police lie to suspects. They may say there's strong evidence when there is none. Or sometimes they beat suspects. Or they refuse them food, water, or sleep. Sometimes they force suspects to confess. Then the "confession" is used against the suspect in court.

Another reason for wrongful conviction is prosecutorial misconduct. That's when prosecutors become overzealous about doing their job. They want to win at all costs. Sometimes they withhold evidence. They mislead witnesses. Or they put prison snitches on the stand. Inmates will sometimes lie in exchange for a reduced sentence.

Bad science is a problem too. Forensics labs get pressure from prosecutors. So they cut corners. Evidence is handled incorrectly. Testing may be done with outdated methods. Forensics labs are sometimes overloaded with too many cases. Or technicians are poorly trained.

These are just a few of the problems that can make our court system unfair. As a result, many innocent people go to jail—or worse, are executed.

The Innocence Project helps to correct unjust outcomes. Lawyers, professors, and law students help the Innocence Project. They review thousands of prisoner letters. They help find prisoners they believe are innocent. They do the legwork. Then the lawyers file appeals. Or they request DNA tests. If needed, they represent the client in court.

Getting help for DNA exonerees is also a priority for the Innocence Project. Some states don't offer any help at all to these former prisoners. In other states, they can sue for financial compensation (money). Currently, only 27 states offer compensation. In other states, there is none.

A guilty prisoner out on parole fares much better than an innocent one. Parolees get some forms of assistance, such as money, clothing, and

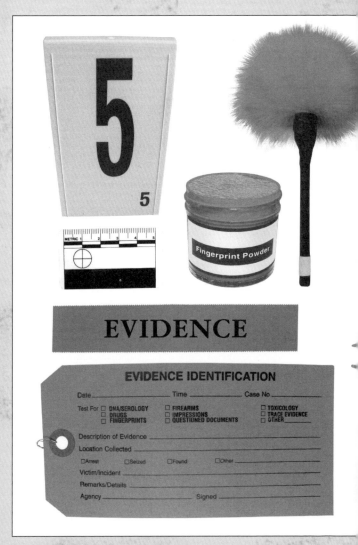

EVIDENCE

EVIDENCE IDENTIFICATION

Date _____ Time _____ Case No _____

Test For ☐ DNA/SEROLOGY ☐ FIREARMS ☐ TOXICOLOGY
☐ DRUGS ☐ IMPRESSIONS ☐ TRACE EVIDENCE
☐ FINGERPRINTS ☐ QUESTIONED DOCUMENTS ☐ OTHER _____

Description of Evidence _____

Location Collected _____

☐ Arrest ☐ Seized ☐ Found ☐ Other _____

Victim/Incident _____

Remarks/Details _____

Agency _____ Signed _____

These items are from a forensic investigation kit for evidence collection and preservation. Investigators look for anything biological: blood, fluid, hair, skin, bones, sweat,

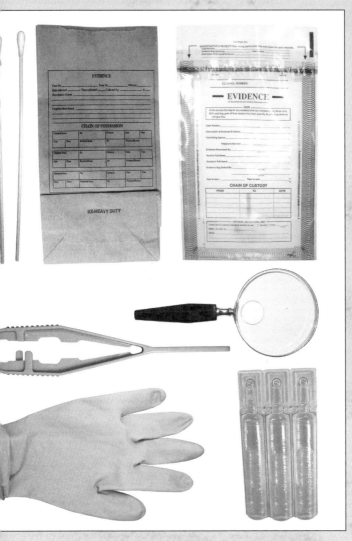

fingernails, urine, and more. They must take care not to contaminate the crime scene with their own biological material, like a single hair or a drop of sweat.

transportation. An exoneree gets none of these. The Innocence Project is working to change that.

Another thing the Innocence Project does is work to preserve evidence. In some states evidence may be destroyed after a time. With DNA evidence destroyed, an innocent person's case is doomed.

Videotaping interrogations is also important. An interrogation is when the police question a suspect. Videotaping protects both sides. There may be a small detail that later becomes important. The videotape catches it. And it keeps the police from having to take notes. They can concentrate on asking questions. So the Innocence Project works on getting videotaping laws passed.

The Innocence Project is working hard to fix the justice system. Thanks to its efforts, many Americans are changing their views on the death penalty, too.

Columbia Law School recently published an article about an unjust execution. The article discussed a prisoner executed in Texas in 1989. It is one of several cases where it is clear that an innocent man was put to death.

The case was based on mistaken identity. The witness said Carlos DeLuna was the killer. But it was later proved that Carlos Hernandez was the killer instead. The two men looked alike. The witness had seen DeLuna handcuffed in the police car. So he said DeLuna was the killer.

DNA evidence proved the witness wrong. An innocent man was killed for a crime he did not commit.

Innocence Project co-director Barry Scheck hailed the Columbia Law School article. He said it showed that this case joined others in which innocent people were executed. The evidence proving DeLuna innocent could help change the law and overturn the death penalty.

CHAPTER 7

Endangered Species of the Gulf
DATAFILE

Timeline

January 1991
Iraqi military releases 240 million gallons of oil into the Persian Gulf to keep US Marines approaching.

June 3, 1979
Oil well Ixtoc 1 explodes in Gulf of Mexico spewing 140 million gallons of oil into the sea.

April 20, 2010
An explosion on the oil rig *Deepwater Horizon* kills eleven.

Where is the Gulf of Mexico?

HERE

Key Terms

dispersant—a chemical that breaks up oil spilled on water

endangered species—an animal whose population is in danger of dying out

gush—a rapid stream or burst

migrate—moving from one region to another

Did You Know?

The piping plover is a small shorebird, only seven inches long. They nest in the Great Lakes, the Northern Great Plains, and the Atlantic Coast. And they spend the winter along the Gulf Coast.

Endangered Species of the Gulf

It was the worst accidental oil spill in history.

Crude oil spewed from the ocean floor. More than 53,000 barrels a day gushed into the Gulf of Mexico. A barrel of oil equals 42 gallons. That's over two million gallons a day. And it gushed for three straight months.

It all started when the *Deepwater Horizon* blew up on April 20, 2010. This huge mobile oil rig was leased by BP, formerly known as British Petroleum. BP is the fourth-largest company in the world.

Hyundai Heavy Industries of South Korea began building the rig in 1998. It was delivered in 2001. It could operate in water 8,000 feet deep. And it could drill down 30,000 feet. That's several miles below the ocean floor.

The rig was about 40 miles from the Louisiana coast when it blew. Engulfed in flames, it burned for 36 hours and then sank. Efforts to put out the fire were unsuccessful.

When the *Deepwater Horizon* exploded, 11 workers were killed. Another 17 were wounded. But that was just the beginning. What came next was an environmental catastrophe.

The rig had been drilling for oil when it exploded. When it sank, the drill broke off. There was nothing to cap the well at the bottom of the Gulf. Oil started gushing out into the water.

Engineers worked on the gushing underwater oil well for three months. Finally, they stopped the leak. But during that time a tremendous amount of oil spilled into the Gulf. Experts say the total spilled could be more than five million barrels.

Huge plumes of oil developed in the water. Some were as much as 22 miles long. Black tar started to wash up on beaches.

So BP started using dispersants. These harsh, toxic chemicals break down the oil. But scientists say dispersants are even harder on wildlife than oil. They cause mutations, or birth defects.

The real victims of the BP oil spill are sea animals. In the six months after the spill, more than 8,000 were found injured or dead. It is predicted that many of the Gulf Coast wildlife species will struggle for years to come.

Environmental workers began helping animals after the spill began. They rescued many wild birds covered in tar, for instance. They cleaned these birds up and released them back into the wild. But many animals continue to suffer.

One of the hardest hit was sea turtles. Five of the world's seven sea turtle species live, migrate, and breed in the Gulf of Mexico. Many sea turtles were endangered even before the oil spill. Sea turtles take 10 to 30 years to mature.

After the spill, the annual rate of sea turtle death was four to six times the average. A lot more sea turtles were dying than normal.

People worked hard after the spill to help sea turtles. One species, the loggerhead, was especially hard hit. The workers moved many loggerhead nests, with more than 15,000 baby turtles. When the babies were old enough, they were released.

Bottlenose dolphins are another species greatly harmed by the spill. Stranded dolphins have been washing up on beaches. Dead or in poor health, they suffer from liver and lung disease.

When oil settles at the water's surface, toxic fumes form above it. Dolphins would break the surface to breathe. When they did, they breathed in toxic fumes.

Did you know that there are more loggerhead turtles in US waters than any other sea turtle? The loggerhead is the largest hard-shelled sea turtle. Adults grow to an average weight of about 200 pounds and an average length of

three feet. Some weigh over 1,000 pounds! Loggerheads love to eat jellyfish, conchs, crabs, and fish. The logger-head is a threatened species.

The toxic chemicals also get into dolphins' bodies when they swallow water. And, they are at the top of the food chain. They eat whole fish. So they consume a lot of toxins that way too.

Coral reefs were also severely damaged by the spill. Reefs are structures built by corals out of calcium. Coral reefs shelter as much as 25 percent of marine life. They are places where small fish and other sea life can hide from predators.

A coral reef seven miles from the spill was ruined by the oil. The reef, as big as half a football field, is dying. There's nothing left but loose coral skeletons covered in mucus and oil.

Many bird species were harmed as well. The brown pelican had just been removed from the endangered species list. The BP oil spill put it in danger again.

Migratory shorebirds were also affected. The piping plover is a good example. This small, sand-colored shorebird is endangered.

Hundreds of species of songbirds migrate every year. Birds such as warblers, orioles, and swallows fly 500 miles nonstop. After wintering in Central and South America, the birds fly north in the spring and early summer to breed in eastern North America. Smoke from the explosion may have altered their migration patterns.

Fish that were harmed include the bluefin tuna and gulf sturgeon. Sawfish are close to extinction, and the BP oil spill made it worse.

It will be years before the Gulf Coast recovers. Some species may be gone for good. We can only hope there is never another oil spill like this one.

CHAPTER 8

DogTown
DATAFILE

Timeline

1976
Dog fighting is finally illegal in all 50 states.

1980s
Best Friends Animal Society establishes its sanctuary at Angel Canyon, Utah.

April 2007
Over 70 dogs—mostly pit bull terriers—are removed from Virginia property owned by NFL quarterback Michael Vick.

Where is Utah?

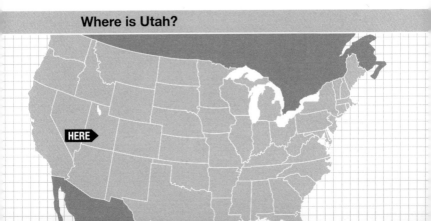

HERE

Key Terms

aggressive—making assaults or attacks

endorsement—approval or permission/sanction

fine—a sum of money paid for an offense or crime

parasite—an organism (animal, plant, bug) living in or on a host

?

Did You Know?

The pit bull is a cross between a terrier and a bulldog bred in 19th century Britain. The pit bull was originally bred as a fighting dog. But today the pit bull is known to be a great family pet and a hard-working farm dog.

DogTown

DogTown is a place in southern Utah. But it's much more than that. It's a place where homeless dogs gain a new lease on life.

The Best Friends Animal Society is a 33,000-acre animal shelter in Utah. There, homeless pets are cared for with love. Best Friends is the largest no-kill shelter in America. That means they don't euthanize pets. They don't "put them to sleep."

DogTown is the canine section of Best Friends. Dogs live there in a kind of doggie village. They get vet care, exercise, and grooming. Injured dogs are nursed back to health. And dogs with behavior problems are trained.

Best Friends CEO, Paul Berry, said, "I've never met a dog we couldn't make some progress with. And most of the dogs, we make very good progress with."

Best of all, the dogs get love and affection. Many of them have been abused. They have never known love. But they find it at DogTown.

After Michael Vick's arrest, some of his fighting pit bulls were sent to DogTown. These dogs were in very bad shape. Most were injured or sick. And they all had behavior problems.

Michael Vick was the quarterback of the Atlanta Falcons. He and some partners owned the Bad Newz Kennels. They bred and raised pit bulls to fight. The dogs were kept chained up. They were horribly abused.

Dogfighting is illegal and cruel. People do it for gambling and excitement. Two dogs are put into a pit. They fight, often to the death. And people crowd around to watch. They make bets on which dog will win.

The Bad Newz Kennels operated for five years in the Virginia woods. Michael Vick paid for it. Buildings were painted black so the dogfights could not be seen at night.

In 2007, Bad Newz Kennels was raided. Authorities removed 53 pit bulls. Some of them were put into foster homes. But 22 of the dogs were so bad off that they were sent to DogTown.

Authorities also found the bodies of a number of dogs that had been killed. These dogs weren't very good fighters. So Michael Vick's men killed them. The dogs were shot, hanged, drowned, or electrocuted.

Michael Vick pleaded guilty. He was sent to prison for two years. And he was fined nearly a million dollars. He lost his endorsement deals, including Nike. It cost him a lot of money.

Part of Michael Vick's fine was used to fund new facilities at DogTown. The 22 pit bulls sent there after Vick's arrest needed a lot of care. Each dog had to have its own dog run so the dogs wouldn't fight. They needed lengthy training, too. It was a huge task.

The National Geographic Channel ran a TV series called DogTown. The show told heartwarming stories of DogTown dog rescues.

In season 2 of DogTown, the Michael Vick story was told. Episode 1, "Saving the Michael Vick Dogs," highlighted four of the rescued pit bulls. They were given new names at DogTown: Cherry, Meryl, Georgia, and Denzel.

Cherry was very shy and timid. He was probably used as a "bait dog." That's a dog that champion fighters practice on. Cherry was so afraid of people that he just cowered. He couldn't even be walked on a leash. He had to be carried. His trainer worked with him for a long time. By the end of the show he was sweet and friendly.

The court ordered that Meryl could never be adopted. She had been aggressive toward people. But she, too, responded well to DogTown training.

Georgia was a former champion who had no teeth. At first the trainers thought she had lost them fighting. But then the vet X-rayed her gums. There were no bone fragments. The teeth had been cleanly removed.

Georgia also had a very saggy belly. It was obvious that she had had many litters of puppies. The DogTown vet figured out why her teeth had been pulled. It was so she could be bred with a male pit bull without her biting him. She was bred with champion males to make champion puppies.

Denzel was sick from the time he got there. He had very low energy and pale gums. The vet figured out he had a parasite called *babesia*. It is passed from one dog to another via dog bites. It is incurable. But the vet was able to treat it and make Denzel feel better.

It turned out that 13 of the dogs had the *babesia* parasite. The dogs had to be kept separate from other dogs.

As for Michael Vick, eventually he returned to professional football. When he was convicted, the Atlanta Falcons kicked him off the team. But after he got out of prison, he went to play for the Philadelphia Eagles.

The American Pit Bull Terrier

1. In the eyes of the American Kennel Club (AKC), the American Pit Bull Terrier is not the same dog as the American Staffordshire Terrier.

2. The pit bull is a muscular, athletic dog. These high-energy dogs must be exercised, and they respond very well to obedience training.

3. Pit bull males can weigh up to 70 pounds (or as little as 30 pounds) and be as tall as 22 inches.

4. The pit bull was brought to the US in the early 19th century by Irish immigrants. It was one of the most popular dogs at the time.

5. Laura Ingalls Wilder's family owned a pit bull. Theodore Roosevelt and Helen Keller also owned pit bulls.

6. Many cities and towns in the US and Canada have banned people from owning pit bull dogs. Some airlines also prohibit the dogs from flying on their planes.

accusation—a charge of wrongdoing; a statement that someone is to blame

activist—a person who works for a cause

aggressive—making assaults or attacks

alpha female and alpha male—the strongest female and male in a pack

committee—a group that works together to accomplish a goal, such as saving a building

condemn—to judge as guilty or unfit

confess—to admit to a crime

desperate—without hope; worried

dispersant—a chemical that breaks up oil spilled on water

DNA—an acid that carries genetic information in a living cell

endangered species—an animal whose population is in danger of dying out

endorsement—approval or permission/sanction

evidence—something that helps prove or establish a point in question

exoneree—a person freed from blame

expert—a person who knows a lot about a topic

fine—a sum of money paid for an offense or crime

gush—a rapid stream or burst

hysterics—a severe attack of panic or distress

innocent—not guilty

landmark—a building or place that is historic or important

media—television, newspapers, and radio

migrate—moving from one region to another

misconduct—unacceptable behavior

municipal—having to do with local or city government

pack—a wolf's family group

parasite—an organism (animal, plant, bug) living in or on a host

press conference—a collective interview where a person answers questions from members of the press

property—things that a person owns

prosecutor—a government lawyer who tries criminal cases

public defender—a lawyer employed with public money to represent a defendant who cannot afford to pay

pup—a baby wolf

rancher—someone who raises livestock

regurgitate—to vomit up food to feed young animals

slated—chosen for a specific purpose

torture—inflicting pain or hurting someone so that he or she will confess or give information

tree-sitter—an activist who climbs a tree and stays up there to keep the tree from getting cut down

vegetarian meals—meals without meat